Glorious Living!

Sowing the Seeds of Enlightenment into Your Daily Life

By

Steve Morris

Teach Your Children Well

You, who are on the road,
Must have a code that you can live by
And so, become yourself
Because the past is just a good-bye.

Teach your children well
Their father's hell did slowly go by
And feed them on your dreams
The one they pick, the one you'll know by.

Don't you ever ask them why
If they told you, you will cry
So just look at them and sigh
And know they love you.

And you, of tender years,
Can't know the fears that your elders grew by
And so, please help them with your youth
They seek the truth before they can die.

Teach your parents well
Their children's hell will slowly go by
And feed them on your dreams
The one they pick, the one you'll know by.

Don't you ever ask them why
If they told you, you will cry
So just look at them and sigh
And know they love you.

Crosby, Stills and Nash

To the gardeners who nurtured me with love;

Sowing my seeds and pulling my weeds:

Don, Pat, Robert, Dorothy, Brayzier and Rheba.

And to Sharon,

My own glorious living gardening mate,

And our four seeds of love:

Ryan, Kaelen, Allison, and Devon.

LotusBloom

A Glorious Awakening

Published by LotusBloom
www.lotusbloom.com

Printed in Singapore by Imago

Color Separation by COLOURSCAN

Cover, layout, and illustrations by Nurbakyah Md Shaw

ISBN: 981-04-4672-1

Glorious Living!
www.gloriousliving.org

Contents

Acknowledgements
Appreciate the kindness of others

express gratitude · offer recognition

praise · regard · admire · commend

affirm · invoke · give thanks

value · appreciate

A great river is the result of many little drops.

Chinese Proverb

The glory of great men
should be measured by the means
they have used to acquire it.

François de la Rochefoucauld-Liancourt

Prosperity makes friends and adversity tries them.
A true friend is one soul in two bodies.

Aristotle

I am wealthy in my friends.

William Shakespeare

So long as we are loved by others
I should say we are almost indispensable;
and no man is useless while he has a friend.

Robert Louis Stevenson

You cannot do a kindness too soon,
for you never know how soon will be too late.

Ralph Waldo Emerson

The initial idea for a book of this sort came from one of my 'student-teachers', Winston Mah, a senior corporate executive whom I was coaching to become a more influential leader.

After many sessions together, Winston expressed the view that it would have been particularly helpful if the self-discovery process which I had guided him through were to have been made available to him when he was younger, before he became inundated by the corporate and material world.

I recognized at once that Winston's suggestion had considerable merit. It was true that many of the questions that I raise with executives are just as relevant to kids, and for that matter to people of all ages. With Winston's inspiration, I endeavored to craft a 'lessons learned' guidebook to serve as a beacon for others, especially those in search of their higher self.

For a logical and spiritually sound foundation on which to erect this beacon, I turned to some of my 'life teachers' for inspiration and guidance, principally: His Holiness the Dalai Lama, Thubten Namdrol Dorje Rinpoche, Venerable Thich Nhat Hanh, and Venerable Tarthang Tulku.

While inspired by great spiritual teachers, this book contains no controversial aspect of faith or religion other than my steadfast belief that we exist for a purpose and that purpose is to find our own inner peace by bringing happiness and well being to others.

My hopeful intention herein is to inspire and enable you to adopt and master the thoughts and behaviors that will subtly, but ultimately, strengthen your inner self while leading to the balance and alignment of your mental, physical, psychological, and spiritual self.

I cordially invite you to enjoy this book, learn something new, and use it to serve others, thereby creating a truly glorious life!

Glorious Living! was fashioned by many hands and many hearts. To my family, friends, clients, and colleagues who encouraged and supported my humble attempt to share that which I have learned to be truly valuable, I wish to offer my heartfelt gratitude. I also wish to thank my editor, Susan Gittins, for her keen ability to correct my imperfect attempts at written communication. Lastly, I especially wish to thank the artist Nurbakyah for her illustrations and layout that inspired me to even higher peaks. 🌸

Introduction

Survey the landscape

I offer this book to you as a *Gift of Glorious Living.*
It contains 280 easily actionable ways in which to improve and
enrich your life. *Glorious Living!* can serve as your holistic guide
for sowing and reaping a perpetual harvest of happiness and
well being.

    Colorful and eye-catching designs and illustrations beckon
you to casually flip through its pages in curious exploration.
An easy-to-read layout invites you to read on and discover more
about yourself while you explore its contents further.

    The book itself is laid out in three main parts: a beginning,
a middle, and an end - each part containing several
four-panel sections.

The front sections will take you through the preparatory stages of growth and development - understanding the context, establishing goals, developing the motivation for change, clarifying needs, expectations, and planning for change. The holistic framework for self-development and self-realization is laid out in *The Gardens of Glorious Living – Learn, Serve, Enjoy, and Bestow.*

The middle sections present the basic guidebook for *Sowing the Seeds for Glorious Living* through the practice and mastery of *28 Bountiful Behaviors.* Simple and straightforward actions and activities are offered as *Seeds to Sow* into our daily lives. The *Seed Actions* are laid out in tabular form to encourage you to glance through and choose items of relevance to your own unique developmental needs and to serve as a tool for ready reference and review.

The back sections are meant to remind you that, like all gardens, *The Gardens of Glorious Living* must be worked and cultivated diligently to produce a bountiful harvest. Suggestions are given to help sustain, develop, and renew you on your journey of becoming.

At the very end is found an abbreviated two-page guide to *the 28 Bountiful Behaviours* and *The Gardens of Glorious Living* as well as a glossary containing nearly 500 *Seedwords* for you to incorporate into your daily vocabulary. How we behave is in large part a reflection of how we speak and think. We can reprogram our behavior through changing our speech.

To introduce and illustrate the meaning of each section, a keyword, a phrase, and some related words and quotations and proverbs are given. A short narrative of explanation and some advisory actions are offered to complete each four-panel section.

Sections can be read and explored individually, at random, or in sequence, from beginning to end. Taken in sequence, the sections tell the story of how *The Seeds of Glorious Living* awaken, develop and grow, ultimately yielding a bountiful harvest reaped from the efforts of diligent and mindful cultivation. After the harvest comes reflection and renewal, a chance to restore and regenerate life.

The harvest cycle is a metaphor for our own cycle of continuous growth and development. By understanding the natural cycle of development and its linkage to happiness and well being, readers of all ages will be better equipped to guide themselves on their individual journeys of growth and self-realization. I hope that this includes you. I invite you to dig in and enjoy the fruits of *Glorious Living!*

Genesis

A seed is planted

origin · catalyst · source

dawn · preface · advent · begin

originate · initiate · conceive · inception

overture · cause · condition

I begin where the last man left off.
Thomas Alva Edison

———— 🫘 ————

The main purpose of life is to live rightly,
think rightly, act rightly.
Mahatma Gandhi

———— 🫘 ————

Be glad of life because it gives you the chance to love
and to work and to play and to look up at the stars.
Henry van Dyke

———— 🫘 ————

Every person bears the whole stamp
of the human condition.
Michel Eyquem de Montaigne

———— 🫘 ————

As we are constituted by nature,
there is not a fault that could not turn into a virtue,
not a virtue that could not turn into a fault.
Johann Wolfgang von Goethe

———— 🫘 ————

The true paradises are paradises lost.
Marcel Proust

———— 🫘 ————

To be what we are, and to become what
we are capable of becoming, is the only end in life.
Robert Louis Stevenson

Balance is our natural state. When we are in balance we radiate confidence, contentment, and comfort. We feel in tune with our natural ability to be energized and comforted by the cosmos.

In an out-of-balance state we feel stress, insecurity, wide emotional swings, and low self-esteem. We feel de-energized and depleted and can even at times be overcome by our own self-generated feelings of despair.

Many, if not most, adults have fallen out of balance at some time or another. Children too are losing their balance. When they enter the socialization process children start to lose their natural sense of 'life balance'.

From school days through to retirement years, our social institutions tend to force-fit our alignment with society at a physical and material level, leaving us feeling disconnected at the spiritual level. Of course, we cannot exist independently of external sources of energy and information, hence we grow to feel an 'imbalance'.

A glorious life awaits those who can find a genuine path of reconnection. To reclaim our balance we need to first recognize the excesses and distractions that are pulling us off-center. We can then reset our directions and realign our behaviors.

Just as a balanced diet and regular exercise lead to good health for our body, a well-balanced heart and mind exercised daily will lead to a healthy and happy life.

Some people have found their places of worship, personal reflection, and meditation to be their personal oases for spiritual reconnection in the desert of self-centered materialism that surrounds us. For many, however, it is difficult to reach these oases without passing through the religious beliefs and dogma associated with them.

Whoever you are, take gladness and inspiration in knowing that we each have our own gardens for spiritual development lying inside us waiting for the *Seeds of Glorious Living* to awaken, blossom, and bear fruit. 🐦

Inspiration

Awaken the seeds within

intent · aim · excite

inspire · spur · vitalize · animate

rouse · motivate · spark · impel

activate · cause · enliven

Even the highest towers are built from the ground.
Chinese Proverb

We all live under the same sky,
but we do not have the same horizon.
Konrad Adenauer

Never, never, never, never give up.
Winston Churchill

Footfalls echo in the memory.
Down the passage, which we did not take.
Towards the door we never opened into the rose garden.
T. S. Eliot

Glory lies in the attempt to reach one's goal
and not in reaching it.
Mahatma Gandhi

Unrest of spirit is a mark of life.
Karl Menninger

You cannot choose your calling.
Your calling chooses you. You have been blessed with
special skills that are yours alone. Use them, whatever
they may be, and forget about wearing another's hat.
Og Mandino

The *Seeds of Glorious Living* exist within each of us. One of these seeds is the desire to fulfil a noble purpose. You may already know this or you may be struggling to connect with it. Either way, a purpose exists and is part of who you are and who you will become. Simply knowing your purpose brings great comfort and confidence.

Glorious

magnificent · extraordinary

elegant · beauty · splendid · sublime

splendor · brilliant · gorgeous

We share the desire for happiness and the aversion of suffering with all living beings. Ironically, we can only achieve lasting happiness, if we let go of our self-centered approach to gaining it. The key to unlocking the secret of our individual happiness lies in others. When we bring happiness to others, we bring happiness to ourselves. This is *Glorious Living*!

Perhaps you have already discovered your seed of inner purpose. If so, have you nurtured it to its full and glorious state? If not, what is holding you back? Are you still struggling to find this seed?

Either way, your *Seeds of Glorious Living* within will still beckon for the earth, water, and sunlight they need to grow and blossom. If your inner purpose still eludes you, read on, the path ahead is well marked with opportunities for rediscovery.

Living

real · alive · aware

active · vibrant · lively · energetic

healthy · potent · vigorous

Infinite possibilities for growth and realization are open to you once you have reestablished a sense of purpose and direction. Begin by allowing yourself to reflect and reconnect to your sense of inner sense of purpose. Your own seeds will awaken through your aspiration to bring *glorious living* to yourself and others.

Aspiration

Arouse a desire for new growth

dream · hope · will

set one's sight on · ambition · yearn

want · wish · desire

reach for the stars · drive

Living without aspirations
is like a boat without a helm.
Chinese Proverb

Lord, grant that I may always desire
more than I can accomplish.
Michaelangelo

Even if you're on the right track,
you'll get run over if you just sit there.
Will Rogers

Only those who will risk going too far
can possibly find out how far one can go.
T.S. Eliot

A man's reach should exceed his grasp.
Or, what's a heaven for?
Pope John Paul I

Wings are essential to a bird;
ambition is essential to a man.
Chinese Proverb

Some men see things as they are and ask why.
I dream of things that never were and say, why not?
George Bernard Shaw

We know that happiness and well being are worthy and worthwhile destinations. From there we can more readily become our fully realized, higher self, drawing ourselves even closer to that which we ultimately seek - a higher state of being, existence, and of realization.

To begin our journey, we must generate a strong and steadfast conviction to reach our destination. We must aspire to become that which we wish to be!

Our aspirations are our passion to struggle, to grow, to reach upward, forward, and outward. Without an aspiration to grow and develop, we become idle, stale and will eventually decay, dissolve and die, unmoved and uninspired.

By extending our reach and raising our aspirations we transform hope into reality; decay into growth; death into life; and unhappiness into happiness. Aspirations become the impetus for us to put forth shoots of new growth.

The *Seeds of Glorious Living* are encouraged to develop through our strong conviction that blooming and blossoming are far better than remaining in dormancy. Suppressing or repressing growth leads to deformation and debilitation.

Our self-development is something that we, not others, 'control'. To grow or not to grow is our choice. We must acknowledge and affirm our own ability to grow and blossom without seeking or waiting for permission, authority, or endorsement from others.

Setting your higher self free to grow is like seeding a field with wildflowers - it is best done in rhythm with nature and will grow to become beautiful on its own with very little effort if given the chance.

Our keen aspiration to reach a higher state of realization will fuel our desire for new growth but, before our *Seeds of Glorious Living* can sprout and take root, they must first germinate and crack through their hardened hulls.

Germination

Sprout and take root

accomplish · deed · start growing

generate · advance · develop

further · bud · produce · stir

progress · engage

Deep experience is never peaceful.
Henry James

Put all your eggs in one basket
- and watch that basket.
Mark Twain

First say to yourself that you would be,
and then do what you have to do.
Epictetus

Let him that would move
the world, first move himself.
Socrates

You cannot create experience.
You must undergo it.
Albert Camus

Luck is what happens
when preparation meets opportunity.
Ebner G. Leterman

No one knows
what he is able to do until he tries.
Publilius Syrus

For our *Seeds of Glorious Living* to germinate, they require earth, sunlight, and water - information, energy, and encouragement. The world around us has more than enough information, energy, and encouragement to support our own personal transformation and the realization of all our aspirations, if only we can gain access to these boundless resources.

The seed hulls that have offered us protection in the past are now holding us back from our future growth. We must break through the hulls to reach the soil, the light, the energy, and the information that will sustain our further development. Our past habits, routines, and mindsets have hardened to form a protective hull around our egos.

To break through the hull you must confront your ego-self directly, being prepared to discover a new self-image, a new self-concept, and a new self entirely. By renouncing your current state of complacency and by embracing the need to change and grow, your *Seeds of Glorious Living* will break through their hulls, peeling away from your past ego-self and bringing you closer to your authentic, higher self.

Aspiration alone is not enough to free us; we need the power of action to coax our seeds through their hulls. Action becomes the lever of aspiration: together with a noble purpose and inspired aspiration, action unleashes energy and realizes potential.

Our lives are composed of innumerable actions: smiling, eating, sleeping, working, walking, talking, reading, writing. But how many of these actions are taking us towards happiness? Which ones are leading to stress and which ones are, quite simply, just distractions?

We have control over almost all of our actions although we may have allowed ourselves to become slaves of habit, unaware of the choices we are making by default. Whether you have made a conscious choice or not, what you do is what you are - good, bad or indifferent.

Ultimately, it is your actions that will define you. You can transform yourself by transforming your daily actions. Through your daily actions you can sow the *Seeds of Glorious Living*. 🌳

Transformation
Stretch, reach, grow, and change

metamorphosis · convert · alter
modify · reform · experiment
adjust · evolve · adapt · fashion
become different · transition · change

There is no fruit
that is not bitter before it is ripe.
Publilius Syrus

All changed. Changed utterly:
A terrible beauty is born.
W. B. Yeats

A diamond is a chunk of coal
made good under pressure.
Anonymous

What we steadily, consciously,
habitually think we are, that we tend to become.
John Cooper Powys

We become just by performing just actions,
temperate by performing temperate actions,
brave by performing brave actions.
Aristotle

Everyone thinks of changing the world,
but no one thinks of changing himself.
Leo Tolstoy

An old peg is driven out with a new peg.
Latin Proverb

Happiness and unhappiness are results of our own thoughts and actions. We reap the good results of good thoughts and actions and the bad results of bad thoughts and actions.

By eliminating harmful thoughts and actions and adopting more beneficial ones, we realize our potential for improved health, happiness, and well being. By transforming your harmful behaviors into beneficial ones you will have sown the seeds for your own happiness and well being.

Transform confusion and ignorance into wisdom through learning. Transform apathy and selfishness into compassionate caring through service. Transform stress and excess into ease through enjoying who you are. Transform destruction and greed into giving and graciousness through bestowing gifts unto others.

LEARN • SERVE • ENJOY • BESTOW

These are *The Four Gardens of Glorious Living* - Learn, Serve, Enjoy, and Bestow. Within these gardens we can sow the *Seeds of Glorious Living* of beneficial thoughts and deeds, or *Bountiful Behaviors*, that will yield a harvest of happiness.

To master new behaviors you must practice them. By integrating *Bountiful Behaviors* into your daily routine, you will live out your happiness as you seek it. A perpetual harvest of health and happiness will be yours, transforming your life and realizing the potential of your higher self.

Transformations can be evolutionary as well as revolutionary. All big changes start as small changes and small changes themselves start with big changes. We often desire the results of revolutionary change without first undergoing any preliminary evolutionary changes; however, all change must begin with an initial change.

But when it comes to the development and growth of our higher self, what should we change first? How can we be sure that we are heading in the right direction? To aid you on your journey of personal transformation, you will need a guide - a path to follow.

Guide

Follow the sun, moon, and stars

steer · direct · lead · pilot · way

navigate · enlighten · escort

pilot · safe passage · leave a trail

show the way · usher · shepherd

Better to ask directions twice than to get lost once.
Danish Proverb

You cannot teach a man anything;
you can only help him find it within himself.
Galileo Galilei

Give a man health and a course to steer,
and he'll never stop to trouble
about whether he is happy or not.
George Bernard Shaw

The real voyage of discovery consists not
in seeking new landscapes, but in having new eyes.
Marcel Proust

A journey of one thousand miles
begins with a single step.
Chinese Proverb

I find the great thing in this world
is not so much where we stand,
as in what direction we are heading.
Oliver Wendell Holmes, Jr.

All I ask is a tall ship and a star to steer her by.
John Masefield

We each have an 'inner-gyroscope' that can be used to monitor and restore our inner-balance - pulling us back when we have overextended ourselves; pushing us forward when we have become lethargic; urging us to get up when we have fallen down and to rest before becoming exhausted.

Our inner-gyroscope guides our moral decision-making too, helping us navigate between choices that will effect our ultimate well being and the well being of others.

Your own gyroscope may have fallen into disrepair from under-use or from remaining in prolonged states of imbalance. Do not despair, it can be restored! But you must be prepared to make the effort.

The *Bountiful Behaviors* presented in *Glorious Living!* will renew and recalibrate your own capacity for self-development and growth. In each of the *Four Gardens of Glorious Living* there are seven *Bountiful Behaviors* to develop and master, *28 Bountiful Behaviors* in total.

Since language has a limited capacity to convey complex concepts over cultural and conventional divides, each of the *28 Bountiful Behaviors* is described in multiple ways, through a keyword, a mantra or phrase, synonyms, and quotes and proverbs to help you connect to its fundamental meaning.

Could different words be better understood? Perhaps, but what makes these keywords special, as you will later discover, is that they themselves form a guide for you to remember them by.

For each of the *28 Bountiful Behaviors*, there are *10 Seeds of Glorious Living* to sow. In all, there are *280 Seed Actions* in this book to help you get started on the right path.

Mastering the *28 Bountiful Behaviors* will develop your wisdom, compassion and concentration, simultaneously setting you on a path towards perpetual happiness and well being. Get ready to dig in and discover some doable disciplines and practical guidelines for nurturing your own personal *Gardens of Glorious Living!*

Cultivation

Sow the seeds and pull the weeds

apply · use · play · exercise

way · attempt · try · effort · test

endeavor · train · experiment · refine

rehearse · live by · put to use · develop

The more ploughing and weeding,
the better the harvest.
Chinese Proverb

An ounce of habit is worth
more than tons of preaching.
Mahatma Gandhi

Character is simply habit
long enough continued.
Mark Twain

Men are all alike in their promises.
It is only in their deeds that they differ.
Jean Baptiste Poquelin Molière

The universe is change;
our life is what our thoughts make of it.
Marcus Aurelius

Life consists not in holding good cards
but in playing well the cards you hold.
Josh Billings

We are what we pretend to be, so we must be careful
about what we pretend to be.
Kurt Vonnegut

Develop your new *Bountiful Behaviors* slowly at first, one day at a time by choosing to 'sow and grow' one or more of the *Seeds of Glorious Living* offered for each of the *28 Bountiful Behaviors*. This will help you get started.

Pulling the weeds *to Glorious Living* is just as important as sowing the seeds! The weeds in the *Gardens of Glorious Living* are greed, anger, foolishness, and fear.

Greed is spread by gross materialism and can be checked by simplifying your life and being mindful of your impact on others and the environment. Anger is spread by divisiveness and can be controlled by awareness of others' needs and mindful speech. Foolishness is spread by complacency and delusions and can be stifled with concentration and discipline. Fear is spread by insecurity and can be countered with wisdom and compassion.

All of the weeds can be prevented from spreading and eradicated altogether by developing a pair of helping and sharing hands, a wise mind, and a sympathetic heart. To become a master gardener in the *Gardens of Glorious Living* you must be able to act wisely, respect life and the world you live in, and control your mind.

TEN TIPS FOR TENDING TO YOUR GARDENS OF GLORIOUS LIVING

🌱 Cultivate each of the *Four Gardens of Glorious Living* over alternating weeks.

🌱 Glance through the *28 Bountiful Behaviors* and place a check-mark by the *Seed Actions* you already do.

🌱 Review the *Seeds of Glorious Living* - place a check-mark by *'Seedwords'* that describe you.

🌱 Consider what you could do to further your mastery of that you are already practicing.

🌱 Choose one, two, or three areas for self-development from a review of the unchecked actions above.

🌱 Select any *Seed Action* at random and practice that behavior throughout the day.

🌱 Record your progress in a daily diary, adding your personal reflections and lessons learned.

🌱 Read *Glorious Living!* with your children, parents, or colleagues; revealing how you see yourself and asking for feedback.

🌱 Discuss the *28 Bountiful Behaviors* with someone that you respect and admire, sharing each others' views and exploring ways in which to master them.

🌱 Share your own thoughts and ideas for the daily development of *Glorious Living!* with me *(www.gloriousliving.org)*.

Harvest

Gather the fruits

reap · gather · obtain · collect

glean · accrete · attain · acquire

realize · achieve · complete

actualize · accomplish

The reward of all action is enlightenment.
Bhagavad-Gita

———— ✦ ————

I am not afraid of tomorrow,
for I see yesterday and I love today.
William Allen White

———— ✦ ————

The mere sense of living is joy enough.
Emily Dickinson

———— ✦ ————

By their fruits ye shall know them.
Matthew 7:20

———— ✦ ————

Good has its rewards and evil has its costs.
Chinese Proverb

———— ✦ ————

A contented mind is a perpetual feast.
Ralph Waldo Emerson

———— ✦ ————

One should, every day at least, hear a little song,
read a good poem, see a fine picture, and if possible,
speak a few reasonable words.
Johann Wolfgang von Goethe

Bountiful harvests do not materialize by seeding alone; seeds must be nurtured and weeds must be pulled to allow room for growth. Daily practice is the sun and rain that will bring life and growth into your gardens. The extent to which you practice these *28 Bountiful Behaviors* will determine the yield of your harvest.

The secret of the *28 Bountiful Behaviors* and their ability to produce a bountiful harvest lies in their interconnectedness. By practicing one *Bountiful Behavior*, others are developed simultaneously, eventually producing harvests from all 28!

The immediate benefactors of your practice of *Glorious Living!* are those people around you. They stand to gain a considerate neighbor, a reliable provider, a caring steward, a loyal servant, an ardent rescuer, a strong protector, a patient teacher, a wise mentor, a noble guide, a keen student, a playful child, a true friend, and a loving companion.

Even though others will be beneficiaries of your kind thoughts, words, and actions, the benefits of sowing the *Seeds of Glorious Living* into your daily life are even greater for you! You will bloom and blossom into your authentic self.

THE FRUITS OF GLORIOUS LIVING

- Longer and improved quality of life by reducing stress, anger, anxiety, and regret.

- Greater overall contentment, happiness, health, and well being.

- More nutrients and energy to nurture your authentic self.

- A restored sense of balance.

- An increase in your internal energy and power available for renewal and healing.

- A release and development of your higher self, with a renewed sense of naturalness.

- A simpler, more enriching lifestyle by providing a consistent, holistic, and integrated approach to daily living.

- Greater alignment and connection to others, linking your self-development to the development of others.

- Stronger wisdom, resilience, and confidence.

- A greater capacity to love and be loved!

Reflection

See how you have grown

consider · contemplate · think · muse

notice · discern · recognize · ponder

appreciate · discover · analyze

sense · inspect · look into

In everything, one must consider the end.
Jean de la Fontaine

———— 🖋 ————

Look at the battle you are involved in;
you are caught in it; you are it.
J. Krishnamurti

———— 🖋 ————

When you understand it's foolish
to look for fire with fire; the meal is already cooked.
Wu-Men

———— 🖋 ————

The trouble with the rat race
is that even if you win, you are still a rat.
Lily Tomlin

———— 🖋 ————

The same thing happened today
happened yesterday, only to different people.
Walter Winchel

———— 🖋 ————

This time, like all time, is a very good one
but only if we know what to do with it.
Ralph Waldo Emerson

———— 🖋 ————

Much unhappiness results from our inability
to remember the nice things that happen to us.
W. N. Rieger

There is no reflection without projection. Before reflecting on our efforts and their impact, we must have made an effort in the first place. Reflection without action is idle dreaming. Action with reflection provides an opportunity for growth, development, and learning.

We often immerse ourselves in activity without taking the time for reflection. Perhaps we fear that we will lose out, fall behind, or get lost if we take ourselves 'offline'. Time for reflection is time for elevating our learning as well as time for renewing and re-energizing.

After *Sowing the Seeds of Glorious Living* for a few months, you will be able to take stock of the changes to your disposition, attitude, and effectiveness. Ask yourself "What have I learned? What can I still do differently to grow and improve even more? What works well for me? What is a continual struggle?" Learn from your struggles and successes.

Give yourself regular and ample time for personal reflection. Review your progress and development from a higher field of view that spans time and is unclouded by the emotions of the moment. Adjust your practice accordingly.

REFLECT ON YOUR PROGRESS

 Evaluate whether you are feeling more balanced and able to restore your balance once lost.

 Visit old friends and family - do they notice a difference in you? Did they mention it to you?

 Draw up a list of *Seedwords* that best describe you emotionally and spiritually. Revise your list periodically. Notice any changes?

 Consider your impact on others. Are you creating more benefit than harm?

 Look deeply at yourself in the mirror. Do you recognize your higher self? Somewhat? Not at all? Perfectly?

 Ponder where you are in life and where you want to be. What is holding you back? Dissolve your fear of change.

 Survey your overall impact on the environment. Are you healing more than harming?

 Look back at the last 28 days (or month), the last 28 months (or two years) and, if possible, the last 28 years. Can you discern any patterns in your development?

 Visualize as precious jewels, all of the wealth, health, and happiness you have brought to others. Watch the treasure grow as you practice.

 Check up on your holistic self after *Sowing the Seeds of Glorious Living*. Can you discern a difference? Can others?

Renewal

Reawaken more seeds within

reopen · regenerate · revive · reawake

enliven · replace · reinvigorate · mend

recharge · reclaim · refresh

restore · replenish · new start

It ain't over till it's over.
Yogi Berra

———— 🐾 ————

There is only one thing
which gives radiance to everything.
It is the idea of something around the corner.
G. K. Chesterton

———— 🐾 ————

Such is the state of life that none are happy but by
anticipation of change. The change itself is nothing.
When we have made it, the next wish is to change again.
Samuel Johnson

———— 🐾 ————

We don't remain good
if we don't always strive to become better.
Gottfried Keller

———— 🐾 ————

If you can spend a perfectly useless afternoon in a perfectly
useless manner, you have learned how to live.
Lin Yu Tang

———— 🐾 ————

I like the dream of the future better than
the history of the past.
Thomas Jefferson

———— 🐾 ————

Sleep after toil, port after stormy seas, ease after war,
death after life does greatly please.
Edmund Spenser

At each end there is a new beginning. Our world is a continual cycle of birth and death, new beginnings and new endings, openings and closings, following in fashion the rhythmic beating of our hearts.

Life is renewed and replenished from an unbounded ocean of life energy. Our individual energy is an inseparable part of that ocean, even though we may have convinced ourselves that we exist as a single drop of rain. True, we are drops of rain, but so too are we the soil that catches the rain and the sun that reclaims the fallen drops skyward. As part of the clouds that contain us, we are reborn once more as a single drop of rain.

Vast potential energy resides in everything around you. To tap into that source of energy, simply focus your energy on the needs and aspirations of others. In doing so, your higher selves will connect. Once there, you will never feel alone or powerless again.

Awaken, and you have become infinite and unbounded. You have been reborn as the sunlight and the rain that will awaken the *Seeds of Glorious Living* in others.

How to Reawaken more Seeds of Glorious Living

➤ Reawaken your childlike self. Remember and rekindle your childhood interests - play again.

➤ Hold an open house and invite people you barely know. Dare to extend your circle of new relationships.

➤ Mend your relationships with people who have been upset by you - offer an apology. Graciously accept apologies offered to you.

➤ Make a fresh start. Decide who you want to be and how you want to be seen by others - be that person.

➤ Go on a personal retreat, sabbatical, or pilgrimage - recharge and reconnect to your inner purpose.

➤ Restore your energy levels - give yourself breaks, vacations, and get-a-ways as treats for having improved.

➤ Revive your spirit by visiting places renowned for their radiance of spiritual energy.

➤ Encourage others to embark on the path to the discovery and development of their own higher selves.

➤ Look for and discover the *Seeds of Glorious Living* in others. Offer yourself as sunlight and rain to encourage their awakening.

➤ Recommit yourself to completing your journey on *The Path of Glorious Living!*

The Four Gardens of Glorious Living

Learn
Develop wisdom

Serve
Overcome apathy

Enjoy
Maintain balance

Bestow
Offer yourself

Learn

Develop wisdom

One remains young as long as one can
still learn, can still take on new habits,
can beat contradictions.

Marie von Ebner-Eschenbach

Investigate Phenomena

Explore your connection

awe · **miraculous** · amaze · *open*

curious · wonder · *perceptive*

marvel · unfold · *inquisitive* · **sensational**

embrace changes · **magical** · reveal

If you wish to make an apple pie truly from scratch, you must first invent the universe. *Carl Sagan*

To be surprised, to wonder, is to begin to understand. *Jose Ortega Gasset*

IMAGINATION IS MORE IMPORTANT THAN KNOWLEDGE. *ALBERT EINSTEIN*

I have learned to use the word impossible with the greatest of caution. *Weiner von Braun*

The universe begins to look more like a great thought than like a great machine.

Sir James Jeans

Sometimes I think we are alone in the universe and sometimes I think we're not. In either case, the idea is quite staggering. *Arthur C. Clarke*

This world, after all our sciences, is still a miracle: wonderful, inscrutable, magical and more, to whoever will think of it. *Thomas Carlyle*

 Life and its surroundings are fabulous phenomena. We are the energy of the stars transformed into the energy of love. Despite mankind's continued effort to ascribe a rational and comprehensible explanation to all events, many remain unexplainable, extraordinary - beyond that which can be readily understood.

Fight the temptation to over-explain natural phenomena and simply marvel at their inherent beauty, rhythm, and mystique. Appease your curiosity through the experience of the sensational. Staying close to natural and supernatural phenomena encourages us to remain open to the mysteries around us. With childlike openness, we retain our belief in the impossible and the miraculous.

Seeking comfort in the known, we allow ourselves to be lulled into believing in the ordinary and the explainable. As a result, we tend to develop a strong fear of that which we don't understand. To counter your fear of the unknown, search out what you do not understand and explore your connection to it. This will lead you to an even greater level of understanding and appreciation. ■

SOWING THE SEEDS TO INVESTIGATE PHENOMENA

- Embrace changes - don't cling to the past.

- Remain open and receptive to the amazing.

- Contemplate the interconnectedness of all living (and non-living) things.

- Sharpen your extra-sensory perception.

- Search for marvels.

- Imagine the unimaginable!

- Suspend your disbelief - accept miracles.

- Get close to phenomena - feel and experience them up close.

- Explore your connection to the cosmos.

- Have faith beyond your senses.

Questioning

Challenge conventional wisdom

validate · inquire · test · substantiate

experience first-hand · question authority

confirm · challenge assumptions

debate · verify · prove for yourself

Doubt is not a very pleasant status,
but certainty is a ridiculous one.
François Marie Arouet Voltaire

Strike a drum to make a sound;
debate the truth for it to become evident.
Chinese Proverb

No man really becomes a fool
until he stops asking questions.
Charles P. Steinmetz

The important thing is not to stop
questioning. Albert Einstein

It's not the answer that enlightens,
but the question. *Eugene Ionesco*

To believe with certainty we must
begin with doubting. *Stanislaw I*

Believe nothing no matter where you read it
or who said it, no matter if I have said it, unless
it agrees with your own reason and common sense.
Buddha

To master our own lives, we must develop our own wisdom. To develop our own wisdom, we must establish our own truths. While accepting the wisdom of others helps us to grow initially, eventually we must substantiate knowledge for ourselves. We must prove to ourselves that which we hold to be true.

Truths exist as notions of convenience. A 'truth' can become a standing assumption and as such often leads us to make fixed and erroneous assumptions. Can you recall instances when you were certain that something or other was to be the case when in fact it was not?

We are foolish to accept any knowledge as permanent and unchangeable since all things change, if only by changing their perspective or orientation, or place in time.

Questioning is our antidote for ignorance by assumption or blind acceptance. The purpose of questioning is to understand for one's self, from one's own perspective, that which we will later refer to as our true knowledge and wisdom.

To be unsure is to be learning. To be learning is to be growing. Learn and grow by challenging conventional wisdom. Ask lots of questions. ■

SOWING THE SEEDS OF QUESTIONING

- Challenge assumptions.

- Prove things for yourself.

- Debate conventional wisdom.

- Question authority.

- Ask questions, inquire, and validate perceptions.

- When you think you know why, ask "Why not?"

- Substantiate, verify, and confirm that
  which is important - do not assume.

- Argue the other side with vigor.

- Question your own beliefs from the ground up.

- Doubt that which is certain, ask "Why?"

Understanding

Open your mind

accept · knowing · aware · alert
empathetic · open-minded · appreciate
agree · receptive · cognizant · fathom
non-judgemental · believe · comprehend

Nothing can be loved or hated unless it is first known. **Leonardo da Vinci**

Nothing in life is to be feared. It is only to be understood. Marie Curie

My knowledge is like a drop in a vast ocean of promise. *Tan Sen*

KNOW ONE TRUTH COMPLETELY AND UNDERSTAND ALL TRUTHS. CHINESE PROVERB

Losing an illusion makes you wiser than finding a truth. Ludwig Börne

We can easily forgive a child who is afraid of the dark: the real tragedy of life is when adults are afraid of the light. *Plato*

Wisdom is to the soul what health is to the body. *François de la Rochefoucald - Liancourt*

 True understanding resonates like fine vibrations. It bathes us in warmth and energy and draws us closer to our cosmic connections. Our own true understanding comes from our genuine understanding of others. Misunderstanding on the other hand brings coldness and distance into our relationships - blocking and depleting energies.

When we have lost confidence in everything we begin to gain confidence in ourselves. The more we become convinced that we know something, the less receptive we are to fully understanding it. A beginner's mind is needed throughout - open, receptive, flexible, and attentive. True understanding is a journey, not a destination.

Abandon your efforts to be understood by others. Instead, increase your efforts towards understanding that which surrounds you - the people, the environment, and the cosmos. Deepening your understanding of others will enrich your capacity to love and serve all. ■

SOWING THE SEEDS OF UNDERSTANDING

- Refrain from judgement - suspend your prior assumptions.

- Be like an empty cup - open and ready to receive.

- Remain open to that which you do not at first understand.

- Start from the other's point of view before considering your own.

- Renounce fanaticism and narrowness - do not force others to accept your views.

- Look for the big picture amidst the details.

- Release attachment to your present views - remain open to the views of others.

- Commit to appreciating others - share your appreciation of them with them directly.

- Distinguish between wisdom, intelligence, and knowledge.

- Seek wisdom as a life-long journey - learn and relearn continuously.

Examine Deeply

Reflect and ponder

distinguish · pensive · contemplate

check-up · inspect · ponder · analyze

muse · find · notice · discern

reflect · look deeply · look critically

Men stumble over the truth from time to time, but most pick themselves up and hurry off as if nothing happened.   Winston Churchill

If we begin with certainties, we shall end in doubts; but if we begin with doubts and are patient, we shall end in certainties.

Francis Bacon

Not every bald head belongs to a monk.
Chinese Proverb

Opinion says hot and cold, but the reality is atoms and empty space.
Chinese Proverb

The heart has reasons that reason does not know.   Blaise Pascal

Forced memorization is not as good as natural realization.
Chinese Proverb

A learned fool is one who has read everything, and simply remembered it.
Josh Billings

Appearances are deceiving. Resist the temptation to take comfort from the superficial appearance of good, bad, right or wrong. Look beyond the obvious for a deeper and broader understanding.

Sharpen your powers of concentration and deep reflection. Begin by developing your power of observation. Focus on your surroundings and familiarize yourself with their richness of detail. Widen your observations to explore the interconnectedness of all things. Look beyond the surface of what you see, at the smaller details - at the tiny reflections. Appreciate the subtle nuances and fine vibrations of energy in all things.

The path to the truth is paved with questions and reflections. While something may appear as a singular truth to you, to others it may not. Learn from their doubt, probe deeper into your own understanding. When we examine more deeply, we are better prepared to accept the absence of apparent or absolute truth. All truths are relative.

Pause and reflect before accepting or rejecting knowledge. Probe deeper by repeatedly asking questions: What? Why? How? Where? The more deeply you examine, the more substantive becomes your body of understanding. ■

SOWING THE SEEDS TO EXAMINE DEEPLY

- Take time to reflect - on your day, your week and your life.

- Reflect on your emotions and analyze their causes - recognize emotions as they arise.

- Look into your palm and see your parents, their parents, and their parents' parents.

- Contemplate on and appreciate the needs, aspirations, and the suffering of those you love.

- Check up on your own motivations in everything you feel, think, say, and do.

- Explore and discover the patterns in your life - consider their broader significance.

- Distinguish between relative truth and absolute truth - look critically at what you call truth.

- Look deeply into the hearts of those you love - feel the connection of your energies.

- Experience rivers, mountains, air, animals, and other people from their perspective, not yours.

- Examine objects with mindfulness - take delight in their subtle details.

Non-Ignorance

Learn continuously

learn · *illuminate* · **inform** · search

intelligent · discover · **mindful** · *insightful*

seek wisdom · awareness · accepting

expand · thirst for knowledge

Iron rusts from disuse, stagnant water loses its purity and in cold weather becomes frozen; so does inaction sap the vigor of the mind.
Leonardo da Vinci

The first problem for all of us, man and woman, is not to learn, but to unlearn. Gloria Steinem

When you are through learning, you are through. Vernon Law

Be ashamed for not learning rather than not knowing.
Chinese Proverb

The only thing more expensive than education is ignorance.
Benjamin Franklin

Everyone is ignorant, only on different subjects.
Will Rogers

No one is as poor as he who is ignorant.
Nederim

Our ability to learn, unlearn, and relearn afresh is one of humankind's greatest natural endowments. Through learning we expand our horizons of thoughts, and awareness. However, the ignorance and misperceptions of those who provide knowledge to us inherently limits our true understanding. As we grow and learn, we must re-assimilate our knowledge from each newly attained level of awareness. At successively higher levels of awareness we can see even greater horizons.

Naturally attained wisdom is mined from a destructive-constructive process whereby we reexamine existing knowledge from new perspectives, learning from old thoughts and ideas and forming new ones, similar to the way a city grows by continuous construction, destruction and rebuilding.

Rebuild your knowledge continuously, make each reconstruction a renewal, a development towards an even higher state of awareness and greater wisdom. In this way your commitment to lifelong learning becomes your personal path to enlightenment. ■

SOWING THE SEEDS OF NON-IGNORANCE

- Admit and acknowledge your ignorance and begin to learn anew.

- Learn from mistakes - mistakes are opportunities for learning if you stop and reflect on them.

- Consider and reflect on the impermanence of all things, especially conventional wisdom.

- Accept the ignorance of others - offer learning opportunities rather than fixed knowledge.

- Associate with people who have insight, energy, and illumination.

- Commit yourself to daily self-development and lifelong learning.

- Accept no knowledge as fixed and unchanging - revisit and rebuild your own wisdom from time to time.

- Make a personal act of improvement - one each day, three a day, five a day, etc.

- Be discerning in your choice of thoughts and activities - be mindful of their impact on yourself and others.

- Aspire to your own enlightenment through seeking wisdom and offering compassion.

Concentration

Focus your energy

diligence · *perseverance* · *patience*

attention · *focus* · **training** · **control**

vigilance · *discipline* · **apply** · **direct** · *devote*

consider · *dedicate* · *attentive*

Perseverance is not a long race; it is many short races one after another. Walter Elliott

Practice is the best of all instructions. Aristotle

Genius is one percent inspiration and ninety-nine percent perspiration. Thomas Alva Edison

Patience and time do more than strength or passion. Jean de la Fontaine

The disciplined man masters thoughts by stillness and emotions by calmness. Lao Tzu

If people knew how hard I worked to get my mastery, it wouldn't seem so wonderful after all. Michaelangelo

Walk slowly and you won't fall down; act carefully and you won't make mistakes. Chinese Proverb

 To develop enlightened wisdom we must be able to pierce through the thick clouds of illusion and the ever-growing jungle of distractions that make up our daily lives. To apply single-minded concentration on an object or concept for an extended period of time, we must be able to discipline our thoughts, and actions.

Concentration is our technique for harnessing our energies and the energy around us. Despite the noise and clutter of the modern world we can still focus our mind to be still like the surface of a tranquil lake. Our powers of observation, listening, and everything we do, increase through our concentration. Concentration is our ability to moderate the pace of action and thinking.

Concentration harnesses the energy of the cosmos like a laser beam focuses rays of light into a single beam, magnifying the resulting energy. Without concentration, you are at the mercy of the distractions and diversions around you. With concentration you have the ability and energy to master your destiny. ■

SOWING THE SEEDS OF CONCENTRATION

- Be patient - practice enduring small hardships or inconvenience without complaint.

- Give yourself time for solitude - develop the realization that even in solitude you are not alone.

- Focus your mind on an object (any household object or flower will do) for an extended period of time.

- Catch and release bad and harmful thoughts as they arise - protect the ecology of your mind.

- Concentrate on the rhythm and harmony of your breathing - breathing exemplifies persistence.

- Set time aside each day for meditation training - practice stilling your mind and taming your thoughts.

- Discipline yourself with deadlines and goals to kindle a sense of urgency.

- Make the mundane extraordinary - sharpen your powers of focus and self-discipline.

- Take a 'Zen' approach to something you do - devote yourself to the task with vigor.

- Focus on the features of the world and people around you - get to know their unique details.

Humility

Bow before others

graceful · **modest** · unassuming

thankful · **unpretentious** · *embraces setbacks*

avoids praise · *no boasting* · humble

prostrate yourself · **subordinates self**

Learning without modesty limits one's skills.
Chinese Proverb

If I can be the world's most humble man, then I can be its highest instrument. *Lao Tzu*

Dare to be naive.

R. Buckminster Fuller

The only upright man is he who knows his shortcomings.
Titus Maccius Plautus

See everything; overlook a great deal; correct a little. *Pope John XXIII*

Any man more right than his neighbors constitutes a majority of one.
Henry David Thoreau

Don't bother just to be better than your contemporaries or your predecessors. Try to be better than yourself. *William Faulkner*

 To learn and grow we must retain a sense of smallness and insignificance to all things. From that perspective we attract development. By seeing ourselves as the 'lowest of the low' we look up to all, respecting all, subordinating our naturally selfish thoughts and desires.

Without our pretensions we can assume a genuine, authentic, yet modest outlook towards life and learning. Every act, incident, and interaction can become an opportunity to learn. Everyone we meet then becomes a teacher, a source of greater wisdom for us to tap into, to further our own self-development. We should be gracious and generous in our thanks to others.

Unfortunately, many people seek acceptance and affirmation rather than true empowerment. By humbling yourself you affirm and empower yourself to improve and grow even further. By drawing attention away from yourself, you make others feel more empowered. ■

SOWING THE SEEDS OF HUMILITY

- Reject the concept of a 'perfect self' - seek to improve rather than to perfect yourself.

- Be gracious towards others (praise, yield, bow, stoop, etc.) - treat others as precious gifts.

- Shift attention away from yourself - avoid receiving praise.

- Give thanks for the nourishment and the kindness that others have provided for you.

- Be unassuming in your attitude - 'dress down' from time to time.

- Recognize the good qualities in others.

- Consider yourself the lowliest among others - be thankful for their company.

- Give credit to others, not yourself - no boasting.

- Ask for and learn from the feedback of others (especially those you don't get along with very well).

- Dedicate the merit from your good deeds to the benefit of others.

Serve

Overcome apathy

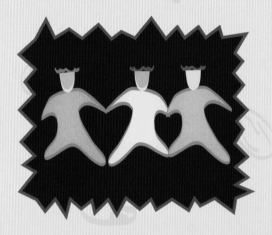

The simplest and shortest ethical
precept is to be served by others as
little as possible, and to serve others
as much as possible.

Leo Tolstoy

Service

Share your compassion

courteous · caring · compassionate
generous · empathize · helpful · dutiful
sharing · volunteer · dedicated
active · meeting others' needs

Only a life lived for others is a life worthwhile. Albert Einstein

He that is greatest amongst you shall be your servant. *Matthew 23:11*

The great man rises above others by lifting up the fallen.
Robert Ingersoll Rand

The wisest course is to think of others when pursuing our own happiness. *Tenzin Gyatso (The 14th Dalai Lama)*

We make a living by what we get, but we make a life by what we give. *Norman MacEwan*

The sole meaning of life is to serve humanity. *Leo Tolstoy*

That service is the noblest, which is rendered for its own sake.
Mahatma Gandhi

 We have many things to be grateful for, not least of which is our ability to help others in need. Those that subscribe to the principle of 'survival of the fittest' are at a loss to explain the propensity of humans to commit purely altruistic acts. Human beings are unique in their capacity to help others for others' sake, without concern for themselves.

We realize spiritual growth through acts of service. It is as if we have helped ourselves by helping others. We need not seek out our service to others, we simply need to be prepared to respond to the many opportunities to serve others that are afforded us each day.

Perhaps the would-be Darwinists would accept the argument that we enhance our long-term spiritual survival through acts of compassionate service for others.

By considering the needs of others in all that you do, you open up additional opportunities to serve. By dedicating your good fortune and good deeds to others, you are elevating the fruits of your energy onto a higher plane. Your service to others becomes its own reward. ■

SOWING THE SEEDS OF SERVICE

- Help instinctively - do not hesitate to lend a helping hand whenever the opportunity presents itself.

- Care for the well being of others - extend your circle of care each day.

- Be active, get involved, avoid idleness - volunteer in service to others.

- Practice non-violence - avoid causing harm or pain to any living beings.

- Be generous with your time and attention - give yourself to others: family, friends, and foes alike.

- Practice compassion by caring, listening, and loving.

- Empathize with others - consider the needs of those less fortunate than yourself.

- Be courteous to everyone you meet.

- Shape your work or daily routine into a service for others.

- Dedicate your efforts to the well being of others.

Harmony

Cherish all equally

cooperation · interdependence

synthesize · fidelity · blend · cherish all

love all · rapport · accord · celebrate · respect

amicable · reconcile · equanimity

If the family lives in harmony,
all affairs will prosper. *Chinese Proverb*

One of the secrets of a long and fruitful life
is to forgive everybody for everything
every night you go to bed. *Anonymous*

Once the game is over,
the king and the pawn go into the same box.
Italian Saying

Many do not know that we are here
in this world to live in harmony.
Buddha

If you judge people, you have no time to love them.

Mother Theresa

Think for yourselves and let others enjoy the right
to do the same. *François Marie Arovet Voltaire*

If a man is gracious and courteous to strangers, it shows
he is a citizen of the world, and that his heart is no island
cut off from other lands, but a continent that joins them.

Francis Bacon

93

 Harmony is a natural state wherein seemingly independent aspects coalesce into an integrated whole. Harmony, once established, becomes a force which deters acts of blatant selfishness.

Harmony is not a collective monotone but rather a rich diversity of individual differences that complement rather than confront and contradict. Harmony is a fine blending of many differing vibrations. Some degree of individuality, however, is needed to extend the robustness, pitch, and timbre of the overall sound. Individuals enrich harmony.

Harmony is a flow, a wave that energizes as it touches and connects with others. We are attracted to harmony and people that are harmonious. It is often our selfishness and our egoism that trip up our ability to harmonize.

Like two lovers in embrace, harmony draws us towards each other, moderating our thoughts, words, and actions to be in tune with those of others. Harmony connects you as a living being to all other forms of energy. Allow your unique vibrations to complement rather than contradict the harmonious whole. ■

SOWING THE SEEDS OF HARMONY

- Establish inner harmony - accept and like yourself and your calling.

- Live mindfully - reduce, reuse, and recycle.

- Be glad for others' good fortunes - celebrate the achievements and successes of those around you.

- Choose to avoid conflict and to reconcile existing conflicts - build rapport.

- Respect everyone and everything, including yourself.

- Do not become attached to outcomes and expectations - be flexible!

- Reflect on the inter-connectivity and interdependence of our world - tune into the cosmos.

- Cherish all equally - love all as you would your own children and parents.

- Play fairly - find win-win-win solutions (where no one loses)!

- Be a role model for cooperation, generosity, and fidelity from today onwards.

Attentiveness

Listen with love

vigilant · alert · compassionate
listening · observant · considerate · courteous
polite · thoughtful · appropriate · calm
cultivate · contemplate · energize

If you wish to see; listen.
Hearing is a step towards vision.
St. Bernard

We have two ears, but only one mouth, so that we may listen more and talk less. Zeno

When I saw something that needed doing, I did it. Nellie Cashman

I have a simple philosophy.
Fill what is empty.
Empty what is full.
And scratch where it itches.

Alice Roosevelt Longworth

The ear is the road to the heart.
French Proverb

Happiness is a by-product of an effort to make someone else happy. Gretta Brooker Palmer

Treat people as if they are what they should be, and you help them become what they are capable of.
Johann Wolfgang von Goethe

 Each being brings to you their richness of heart, mind, and body. They, like you, struggle to communicate and relate with their higher self. Your attentiveness towards them will attract and draw out their higher selves. In this way you can see the nature of your own higher self. Others will experience you as a reflection of your intentions and actions.

Always be alert and vigilant to the needs and gifts of others. Consider everyone as your most precious child and attend to them as such. Sometimes just a compassionate smile or a listening ear is enough to encourage, assuage, and affirm another human being. Extend where you draw the line between 'will and won't' to further your growth as a compassionate companion.

Direct your thoughts, energies, and attention towards others in order to expand your scope, or field of consciousness. Drink often from the fountain of attentiveness as it provides the richness of others' experiences, needs, aspirations, and energies. ■

SOWING THE SEEDS OF ATTENTIVENESS

- Rediscover and reconnect to the meaning in your life.

- Listen attentively when discussing - be an active listener; summarize and ask questions.

- Defuse anger by remaining calm, even while under 'attack'.

- Be vigilant - look ahead with awareness and preparedness.

- Stay alert and 'in the zone' - keep your senses in a state of heightened awareness.

- Cultivate and share your life energy through experiencing the wonders of life.

- Learn and practice applying the right effort at the right time.

- Re-energize yourself by taking periodic energy breaks.

- Look at and listen to others with your heart as well as your mind - be considerate.

- Protect the ecology of your mind - keep it from becoming polluted.

Relief

Relieve suffering

empathize · embrace · sympathize

compassionate · centered-heart

remove obstacles · protect · sensitive

caring · feeling · pity

The greatest tragedy is indifference.
Red Cross Slogan

SOME PURSUE HAPPINESS -
OTHERS CREATE IT.
ANONYMOUS

The worst sin towards our fellow creatures
is not to hate them but to be indifferent
to them; that is the essence of inhumanity.
George Bernard Shaw

What do we live for if it is not
to make life less difficult for each other?
George Elliot

There is no exercise better for
the heart than reaching down and
lifting people up. *John Andrew Holmer*

Better a cold body than a cold heart.
Chinese Proverb

With malice toward none;
with charity for all.
Abraham Lincoln

We may often think and feel that we are powerless to relieve the suffering of others and at times it may seem an overwhelming task and beyond our capacity to help.

We tend to think that we cannot make a difference by ourselves. In fact, quite the opposite is so. There are infinite ways in which we can make a positive difference to people's lives, either directly or indirectly.

By refusing to accept indifference we force ourselves to engage, to react, and to protect. As all living beings are capable of experiencing pain, fear, and suffering, we can relate on a fundamental level to the avoidance and cessation of suffering. Compassionate relief is aimed at removing obstacles without creating suffering for others.

Whatever the current state of your own well being, your efforts to relieve the suffering of others are guaranteed to elevate your own spirit as well as your spirituality. You can make a profound difference in someone's life just by lending a shoulder to lean on. Be ready and willing to respond. ∎

SOWING THE SEEDS OF RELIEF

- Extend your awareness of the suffering of others - appreciate the extent of suffering around you.

- Find ways and opportunities to be with those suffering - seek to relieve their suffering.

- Offer those in suffering a compassionate word, action, or thought.

- Avoid causing suffering or harm to other beings.

- Select a vocation that realizes your ideals of compassion while minimizing harm and suffering.

- Prevent others from enriching themselves from human suffering (or the suffering of other beings).

- Do not kill nor let others kill - protect life and prevent war.

- Exchange yourself with others - sympathize with their feelings and share their pain.

- Acknowledge suffering - do not avoid contact with suffering or close your eyes to it.

- Live and let die - respect both life and death.

Intention

Choose to act

decisive · persistent · enduring

purpose · view · aim · target · deliberate

willful · meaning · resolute · faithful

aspire · hope · positive potential

Be careful what you wish for, it may come true. *Unknown*

If things are not as you like, wish them as they are to be. *Yiddish Proverb*

Everything that is done in the world is done by hope. *Martin Luther*

When you wish upon a star, your dreams come true. *Jiminy Cricket*

To wish progress is the largest part to progress. *Lucius Annaeus Seneca*

Strength does not come from physical capacity. It comes from indomitable will. *Mahatma Gandhi*

Above all, do not lose your desire to walk. *Sören Kierkegaard*

Intention wells up inside us, subtly at first as a seedling of an idea, taking root as an aspiration and blossoming into an invigorating force that will sustain itself to fruition. The formation of intention dissolves the hardened hulls of indifference. Intention is the energy of the cosmos.

Virtuous intentions attract the support of others, enriching their soil and attracting other intentions that will cross-pollinate and mutually support each other.

Reflect upon your interactions with the world. Ask "What am I trying to achieve? What is the outcome I hope to attain? Why is this outcome important to me, or to others? What would my higher self choose to do?"

Do nothing halfway. Choose to act or do not act at all. Become aware of your intentions. Give them a permanent place to reside in your integrity and your purpose. What is material is first immaterial - a child for example begins as an act of intention. Your positive potential is released through your intentions - let them be virtuous ones.

Intention alone does not an orchard make. Strengthen your intention by choosing to be deliberate in your actions. Affirm the choices that you make. ■

SOWING THE SEEDS OF INTENTION

- Examine your motivations and reestablish your intentions - be clear why you choose to do what you do.

- Dedicate yourself to serve others - do something meaningful for others.

- Choose to act - deliberate, decide, and do it!

- Put more meaning into your life and everything you do - affirm the choices you make.

- Be persistent - resolve to develop and extend your endurance.

- Be decisive - take responsibility for your decisions.

- Share your intentions openly - make it easy for people to understand your motivations.

- Replace non-virtuous intentions with virtuous ones - start by being faithful.

- Willfully offer joy and happiness to others - remind yourself of your limitless positive potential.

- Approach others with intention and purpose - do not remain aloof.

Nurturing

Develop others

modeling · *guiding* · mentoring

sustain · *cultivate* · *foster* · *nourish*

educate · **steer** · *show* · *direct* · *support*

pilot · *usher* · *advise* · **stewardship**

JUST AS THE TWIG IS BENT,
THE TREE IS SO INCLINED.
ALEXANDER POPE

**Whatsoever a man soweth,
that shall he also reap.**
Galatians 6:7

*The first great gift we can bestow
on others is a good example.*
Thomas More

*Not even a prairie fire can destroy the grass;
it grows back when the spring winds blow.*
Chinese Proverb

To teach is to learn twice. Joseph Joubert

THE DONKEY ENTRUSTED WITH
RESPONSIBILITY WILL GALLOP FASTER
THAN A HORSE WITH NONE.
TIBETAN PROVERB

The greatest good you can do for another
is not just to share your riches but to reveal
to him his own. *Benjamin Disraeli*

 To nurture is to make ready for new growth. We can contribute to others' growth in many areas: physical, intellectual, social, moral, and spiritual. However, our shaping force must be applied in juxtaposition to our own tendency to become diverted and distracted. You cannot save a drowning child if you are drowning yourself.

Our nurturing role towards others is a giving role, a sharing role - not an imposing role. It is not for us to impose our values and beliefs on others but rather to make them available to guide and inspire. We may seek to direct and steer but ultimately it is others who must choose their thoughts and actions, not us.

Through our leadership example, our positive role modeling and active mentoring, we are offering both our greater and lesser virtues and values to be used by others to affirm or reject as their own.

You need not be perfect or expert in any way. Simply be available to others as yourself. Your reflection in the mind's eye of those you engage will be enough to cultivate a perennial harvest of learning, growth, and development in others. ■

SOWING THE SEEDS OF NURTURING

- Be aware that you are a role model to others - polish yourself up a bit each day.

- Nourish your own self-esteem - reflect on your contributions to the well being of others.

- Assist in the education and development of others - teach, advise, and guide.

- Offer to mentor someone in need of development.

- Give guidelines to others to prevent the development of harmful habits.

- Confront harmful, destructive behaviors - show people alternatives.

- Give kids a good head start - spend time with them as a role model.

- Offer yourself to the development of your local community - volunteer your time to a chosen cause.

- Protect and defend those in need - usher in others to help.

- Be a part-time foster parent, or sibling, or child - adopt or be adopted yourself, at least informally.

Gentleness

Show goodwill towards all

tenderness · goodwill · helping · **benign**
benevolent · yield · defuse · soft touch
kind affection · mild · **tender-hearted**
delicate · considerate · embracing

Always be a little kinder than necessary.
James M. Barrie

In this world you must be
a bit too kind to be kind enough.
Pierre Carlet de Chamberlain

Gentleness, self-sacrifice and generosity are the
exclusive possession of no one race or religion.
Mahatma Gandhi

Gentleness overcomes harshness.
Chinese Proverb

If we find that we cannot help others,
the least we can do is to desist from harming them.
Tenzin Gyatso (The 14th Dalai Lama)

Commonplace love: often it is the only kind
possible...to help others as best you can,
to avoid losing your temper, to be understanding,
to keep calm and smiling (or as much as possible).

Pope John Paul I

 Kindness is as delicate as a dewdrop suspended on a spider's web. The subtleties of our love and compassion are revealed in the gentleness of their application. Kindness begets kindness surely as anger begets anger.

Our compassionate understanding beckons us to embrace others with a heart-felt intention to dissolve their fears, hatred, and insecurities. Being neither too smothering nor too overpowering in our interactions with others will encourage their engagement without fear. With a tender heart, goodwill and a soft touch, gentle people are welcomed among men and beasts alike for they bring the energy and warmth of benevolence and grace. Gentleness is a strong cosmic force, gathering strength from successive acts of kindness and compassion.

A single act of kindness can transform the most treacherous of situations. An authentic smile can be disarming, inviting others to release their weapons of insecurity. If your kindness is genuine and freely offered to all, especially those who seek to anger and harm you, others will be inspired by your example towards greater kindness themselves. Wake up gently each morning and seek to remain gentle throughout the day. ◼

SOWING THE SEEDS OF GENTLENESS

- Demonstrate your goodwill, greet everyone with a relaxed and sincere smile.

- Adopt a positive posture - physically as well as mentally.

- Show kindness and goodwill to all living beings - practice non-violence.

- Speak gently to defuse anger, especially when under 'unrighteous' attack.

- Soften your touch - 'tenderize' yourself, be considerate.

- In a conflict, transform your view - sympathize with your adversary.

- Offer apologies and seek to reconcile with others - offer victory to others by yielding.

- Graciously accept the apologies of others - add your apology to theirs.

- Dissolve anger into forgiveness - practice when you are not angry.

- Embrace softly (hug) everything that you can, while you can!

Enjoy

Maintain balance

We are all happy if we only know it.

Feodor Dostoevsky

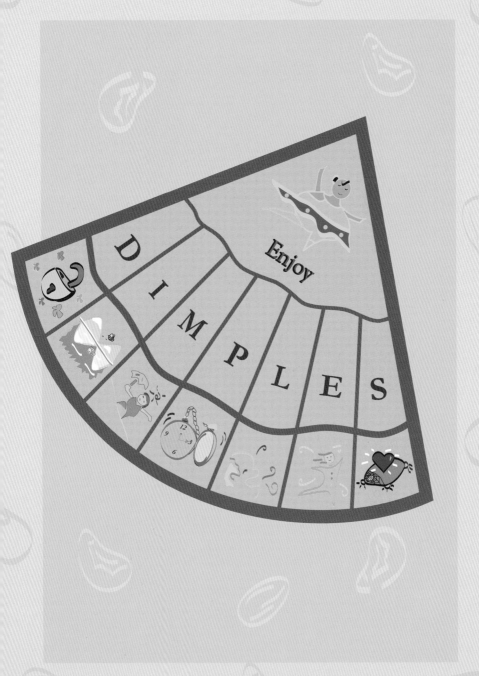

Detachment

Let go

step back · non-grasping

fair · *cool* · *dispassionate* · **neutral**

transcend · *relinquish* · *forego* · *impartial*

unprejudiced · **defer** · *release* · **unlock**

Govern your passions or they will govern you.   *Latin Proverb*

When I am standing on Mt. Lu, I see not the true face of Mt. Lu.
Chinese Proverb

It is the greatest advantage to enjoy no advantage at all.
Henry David Thoreau

Life appears to me too short to be spent in nursing animosity or registering wrongs.
Charlotte Brontë

No man enjoys the true taste of life but he who is ready and willing to quit it.
Lucius Annaeus Seneca

How many people are killed in accidents because of not wanting to let go of their umbrellas?
Paul Valery

 Our greatest risk of downfall lies in the arrogance of our own ignorance. By acknowledging our own fallibility, we loosen our grip on self-validating thoughts and ideas. There can never be a purely impartial view, since all views are colored from the perspective of the individual. Therefore, when it comes to views there can be no right, and no wrong.

Allow that others' views are equally as valid as your own. Welcome diversity of opinions as enlightening in their totality, as the infinite multitude of the rays of light that emanate from the sun.

When we give in to the insecurity of our ego, we become rigid, inflexible, and self-righteous. The stronger our ego, the more at-odds we become with the rest of the world. Our unchecked egos are our greatest threat to universal harmony and ultimately our own lasting happiness.

Continue stepping back to gain a broader and deeper perspective on all things. Step back so far as to endeavor to cross through the physical limits of this spatial existence. From higher dimensions come greater viewpoints and deeper understanding. By letting go of your self-centeredness you become better aligned with the energy of others and can ultimately tap into the full energy of the cosmos. ■

SOWING THE SEEDS OF DETACHMENT

- Separate people from their actions - review events from a neutral perspective.

- Transcend the concept of your 'perfect self' - be less defensive to feedback and criticisms.

- Accept criticisms and negative feedback with thanks.

- Don't hold a grudge - release it! Keep your emotional ledger in balance.

- Let your 'self-centeredness' take the blame and pain for problems and criticisms.

- Yield your position to others from time to time - choose your battles.

- Control your emotional responses - recognize the physical symptoms of anger and other moods.

- Remain impartial to any doctrine, theory, and ideology - they are only guides, not truths.

- Forgive and forget (often) - let go of emotional anger and attachment.

- Forego your prejudices to restore your impartial viewpoint - reset your objectivity.

Inner Stillness

Compose yourself

patience · calm · *peaceful* · *solitude*

still · placid · **clear** · *tolerant*

serene · **tranquil** · composed

non-agitated · unruffled · **pause**

A mind that is fast is sick. A mind that is slow is sound. A mind that is still is divine.
Meher Baba

Silence is the garden of meditation.
Ali

I never found the companion that was so companionable as solitude.
Joseph Addison

How can I become still?
By flowing with the stream.

Lao Tzu

**Without inner peace,
it is impossible
to have world peace.**
Tenzin Gyatso (The 14th Dalai Lama)

The absence of alternatives clears the mind marvelously. *Henry Kissinger*

Silence. All human unhappiness comes from not knowing how to stay quietly in a room. *Blaise Pascal*

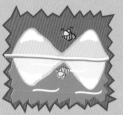 Our minds are cluttered with a multitude of distractions. The noise level within our heads is being raised by the increasing bombardment of the sounds and images of our modern lives.

To defend yourself from the deluge of distractions, develop your ability to switch into stillness. From that vantage, just atop the still surface of your reflective mind, you can peer across the infinite.

Keeping calm is great advice. From a calm state, any response is possible. From an agitated state there are only two: further agitation leading up to an outburst; or sudden de-agitation which can also be de-stabilizing.

By stopping harmful, angry thoughts from arising, you strengthen your ability to respond to situations uncolored by emotions, composed and yet compassionate.

Learn to recognize what disrupts your inner stillness and perhaps more importantly what restores it. Choose to let go of disrupting emotions as they arise. Through mindfulness of action, even one as simple as breathing, you can restore your inner peace. ▓

SOWING THE SEEDS OF INNER STILLNESS

- Set aside time for solitude - use the time to listen, smell, feel, and dissolve all into tranquility.

- Replace habitual anger with habitual patience.

- Practice tolerance with the attitude of sacrifice.

- Pause to remain calm in a crisis - offer your composure to others as strength.

- Re-balance yourself with visits to surroundings that nourish you.

- Develop your ability to sit or stand anywhere and establish momentary peace and serenity.

- Close the window to distractions - simplify your life.

- Store all that agitates, ruffles, upsets or excites you in a mental 'shoe box' - practice putting it aside.

- Focus on breathing mindfully when you feel yourself becoming agitated.

- Compare your calmness over time - inner calmness is attained in steps.

Middle Way

Retain your balance

balance · equalize · center · **modest**
moderate · compensate · no extremes
counterweight · equanimity · equilibrium
intermediate · midway · temper · tame

The moon waxes, then it wanes.
Chinese Proverb

There is no end. There is no beginning.
There is only the infinite passion of life.
Frederico Felini

The pole is easy to carry
if the load is balanced.
Chinese Proverb

The road uphill and downhill
are one and the same. *Heraclitus*

Between two evils, choose neither;
between two goods, choose both.
Tyson Edwards

A lifetime of happiness?
No man alive could bear it.
It would be hell on earth.
George Bernard Shaw

The test of a first rate intelligence is the
ability to hold two opposed ideas at the
same time; and still retain the ability to
function. F. Scott Fitzgerald

 From the true center, all paths are equally distant; similarly, all paths are equally near. From the depths of darkness, dawn arises. All perspectives are relative.

While we prefer to think of light and dark as two separate and opposing concepts, they are in fact inseparably part of a singular concept - the sun - which is governed by the strong nuclear force, which is itself a part of a larger concept, that of the laws of physics, and the universe. Since even opposites are part of the same whole, extremes cannot exist on their own, they must co-exist with an opposing force.

Balance is the state whereby opposing forces are perfectly and truly offset. Caught between two opposing extremes, true balance retains the energy of all forces without succumbing to any one. As such, balance is a source of eternal energy.

To retain your balance you must avoid stepping too far out of the center. While the motionless balance of stillness may impress onlookers, it is static and lifeless. True balance is neither still nor moving; but rather exists in a state of constant flux. Balance, together with movement and life, is the source of all that is graceful. A life of balance is a life of grace. ▎

SOWING THE SEEDS OF MIDDLE WAY

- Avoid excesses and extremes - do everything in moderation.

- Eliminate dualistic concepts - everything is relative. Avoid absolute comparisons - all things change.

- Check up on your own mental projections; they can easily change, be wrong, or be revised.

- Keep your balance - find and return to the center.

- Act and be non-judgmental - avoid putting your own values on others.

- Accept and remain open to everything and everyone - don't discriminate.

- Look for the dawn in the darkest hour (extreme heat can become coolness over time).

- Widen your field of view to reveal the infinite number of midpoints to everything.

- When given only two choices, 'right or left', 'up or down', etc., create a third choice.

- Recognize your extreme views so as to temper them.

Present

Live the moment

now · current · presence · authentic
exists · live · mindful · ready
act naturally · improvise · here and now
be yourself · spontaneous

Each day should be passed
as though it were our last.
Publilius Syrus

Time is the most valuable thing one can spend.
Thespharastus

Today is the first day
of the rest of your life.
Abbie Hoffman

A moment of time is like a piece of gold,
but a piece of gold won't buy a moment of time.
Chinese Proverb

For me, the present is merged in eternity.
I may not sacrifice the latter for the present.
Mahatma Gandhi

There is no distance on
this earth as far away as
yesterday. Robert Nathan

Not knowing when the dawn
will come I open every door.
Emily Dickinson

 From a perfect state of balance, anything, is possible. Achieving balance opens up our ability to be spontaneous. From spontaneity springs forth learning, laughter, and love. Mindful breathing is an effective means of rebalancing our mind and body. Stop. Breathe. Think. Act. Mindful breathing stills the inner storms of our mind. From a calm state we can enjoy the present moment to the fullest as our authentic self, undisturbed by the inner storms.

Be mindful to present yourself to others as your authentic self. Remove the masks we selectively don to protect and entertain our fragile and demanding egos.

Excavate through the layers of unauthentic self, which have been built up over time like sedimentary layers of stone. Remove the last opaque veils of insecurity, delusion, and distrust.

Set aside your own personal agendas and motivations. Simply, be yourself, completely there - not more, not less. Alert and attentive, you can give your full self to the present moment. From there the rest is simple - just improvise and enjoy! ▪

SOWING THE SEEDS OF PRESENT

- Be there, now! Enjoy the current moment to its fullest.

- Do not worry about the future; it may never come.

- Do not cherish regret for the past - it's gone.

- Reset your timeclock - breathe in, breathe out - no past, no future.

- Hug those who are close to you - breathe three times for love as you do.

- Find satisfaction from doing simple tasks and chores well - master the mundane.

- Be ready to respond. Stop. Breathe. Think. Act.

- Give yourself as a 'present' to others who would like to share your time.

- Follow your spontaneous urges - improvise!

- Live with appreciation for life - be thankful for each new moment and experience.

Laughing Joy

Cut loose

amuse · funny · comical · delight

gladness · merriment · ridiculous

humorous · happiness · rejoice · laughing

refresh · express yourself

The sound of laughter
has always seemed to me
the most civilized music
in the universe. *Peter Ustinov*

Humor is an affirmation of dignity, a declaration of our superiority of all that befalls us.
Romain Gary

Joy puts heart into a man.
Chinese Proverb

Cheerfulness is the offshoot
of goodness. Christian Nestell Bovee

Laughter is the sun that drives winter
from the human face. *Victor Hugo*

A merry heart doeth good
like a medicine.
Proverbs 17:22

Great is the human who has not lost his childlike heart.
Mencius

 A smile when worn with sincerity beckons for its own reflection. A smile in times of adversity inspires hope.

Children smile and laugh with ease, spontaneously and without reservation. In this way, children embody the concept of 'cutting loose'. As we mature we learn to hold back, to be reserved and in control.

We have developed our rational reflexes to the extent that we can suppress our natural desire to laugh, to express joy and pureness of being. How completely rational is it for us to 'cut loose' and behave irrationally from time to time? Laughter is a sword that can cut through our excessively rational behavior, an antidote to that which poisons our will to be joyful.

You can test the extent of your own ability to suppress or release '*Laughing Joy*' by considering the most outrageous and out-of-character activity you have indulged in recently. Share your story with someone else. If they can't help but to laugh or giggle, then you are definitely on the right track! ■

SOWING THE SEEDS OF LAUGHING JOY

- Do not take things too seriously - smile in adversity.

- Practice laughing; always laugh when others laugh - laugh first from time to time.

- Remember what makes you happy - keep some, in reserve.

- Express yourself when you are joyful - laugh, giggle, just grin!

- Develop joy in your mind - revisit it whenever you would like, or need, to.

- Touch and rejoice in things that are beautiful and refreshing - inside and outside yourself.

- Find merriment in the mundane - amuse yourself in your daily routine.

- Be glad and smile for the happiness and good fortunes of others.

- Smile early in the day and often after that.

- Delight in the ridiculous from time to time - allow yourself to be easily amused.

Ease

Relax and unwind

simplicity · relax · rest · enjoy

rejuvenate · smile · no worries · **calm**

de-stress · unwind · glide · **refresh** · restore

right tension · let go · **loosen** · comfortable

The sun, with all those planets revolving around it and dependent on it, can still ripen a bunch of grapes as if it had nothing else in the universe to do. *Galileo Galilei*

Everything should be made as simple as possible, but not simpler.
Albert Einstein

If you know the nature of water, it is easier to row a boat. *Chinese Proverb*

By letting go, it all gets done; the world is won by those who let it go! But when you try and try, the world is then beyond winning. *Lao Tzu*

You are never fully dressed until you wear a smile. *Charley Wiley*

Humanity takes itself too seriously; it is the world's original sin.
If the caveman knew how to laugh, history would have been different.
Oscar Wilde

It's very hard to take yourself too seriously when you look at the world from outer space.
Thomas K. Mattingly

 As any roller coaster rider or thrill-seeker will attest, fear and excitement are two sides of the same emotion. It is laughter that breathes lightness into fear - even going so far as to transform fear into excitement.

Relax and let go to fully enjoy each moment. As a child this was easy for us to do; to relax, to laugh, to smile, to enjoy our environment. During our adult lives we tend to become rigid and inflexible, less able to stay relaxed and loose.

By adopting formal roles and wearing the masks of people we are not, and by following rules that lead us to suppress our expression and emotions, we over 'tighten' ourselves, leading to stress and tension. We can prevent ourselves from winding up too tight by learning to unwind, to go with the flow, the true nature of things.

Looking into the calm surface of a mountain lake, we enjoy the reflection of the lake's surrounding beauty. When there are disruptions to this calm state, our view becomes distorted. Similarly, our minds and hearts reflect the beauty of their surroundings when we are calm and at ease.

Start by practicing 'letting go', by accepting situations that you cannot alter. Avoid responding to situations with agitation and anger. This will only further wind you up! Unwind, especially in challenging circumstances. Deep, mindful breathing can be used as a centering technique, affording you an opportunity to recenter, to recharge, and to rejuvenate.

SOWING THE SEEDS OF EASE

- Let go of worrying - if you can do something about the situation, then do. If you can't, why worry?

- Do not retain anger or hatred - transform them into understanding through breathing and patience.

- Pause and unwind to allow yourself time to heal, rest, and rejuvenate.

- Breathe it easy! Practice mindful breathing to transform fear into excitement.

- Restore yourself to a calm (non-agitated) state - reset and relax.

- Accept situations which you cannot alter - avoid anger and agitation, they age you like no other.

- Let angry people calm down before you try to engage them.

- Avoid overcomplicating your life - keep it simple.

- Do not look for fault nor assign blame - take it easy.

- Let it be!

Self-Respect

Like yourself

self-esteem · confidence · courage

affirming · encourage · like yourself

appreciate · cherish · relish

respect · treasure · value · self-accepting

He that respects himself is safe from others. He who conquers himself is mighty. **Henry Longfellow**

Self-respect knows no considerations. *Mahatma Gandhi*

No one can make you feel inferior without your consent. *Eleanor Roosevelt*

If I am not I, who will be? *Henry David Thoreau*

Self-reverence, self-knowledge, self-control. These three alone lead life to sovereign power. **Norman MacEwan**

There is no one else who can ever fill your role in the same way so it is a good idea to perform it as well as possible. *Humphry Osmond*

The most exhausting thing in life, I have discovered is being insincere *Anne Morrow Lindbergh*

 We are simultaneously our own best friend and our own worst enemy. We often tear down our confidence in our abilities and belief in ourselves. How we feel about ourselves is directly reflected in how we feel about and engage with others. When we feel empowered, we help others to feel empowered. The converse is also true, if we have lost confidence or faith we tend to deprive others of theirs.

With a high positive sense of self-respect we are at our best to learn and to grow further. When our self-esteem has been torn down, we are reluctant and reticent to invest in our own growth. How we feel about ourselves is directly related to how well we perform, interact, learn, and relate with others. We are often at our best when we feel as though we are at our best.

To establish your own happiness you must take charge of your own body, speech, and mind, choosing to whom and when to entrust them.

Begin by affirming all of the good in you and all of the good you have offered to others, no matter how insignificant you consider it to be. Affirm also your positive aspirations to further develop and grow on the path to enlightened living. Now, you have become even more precious.

SOWING THE SEEDS OF SELF-RESPECT

- Respect yourself - give yourself the best chance of growing and developing to your potential.

- Be your own best friend; you are certain to have many likeable aspects - like yourself.

- Protect and encourage the esteem of others - help make them feel good about themselves.

- Strengthen your own self-esteem - change how you feel about yourself; encourage yourself with gusto.

- Accept yourself, faults and all - acknowledge and affirm your good qualities.

- Acknowledge your emotions as they arise - do not deny emotions, release them.

- Meditate on how others see and experience you - envy and admire yourself.

- Rid yourself of controlling influences, people, or substances that lead to self-deprecation.

- Blame your ego for your problems, not other people.

- Practice distinguishing your higher self from your daily self - bring the two into convergence.

Bestow

Offer yourself

We are here to add what we can to life,

not to get what we can from it.

William Osler

Transforming

Replace harmful with helpful

convert · revolutionize · change

transition · alter · metamorphosis · commute

vary · adapt · opportunity from danger

transmute · modify · mutate

The soul is born old but grows young.
That is the comedy of life.
And the body is born young and grows old.
That is life's tragedy.

Oscar Wilde

Make it a point to do something new every day that you don't want to do. This is the golden rule for acquiring the habit of doing your duty without pain.

Mark Twain

In the middle of difficulty lies opportunity.

Albert Einstein

When it's dark enough, you can see the stars.

Charles Beard

Suffering cheerfully endured ceases to be suffering and is transmuted into an ineffable joy.

Mahatma Gandhi

TO LIVE IS TO BE
SLOWLY BORN.

ANTOINE DE SAINT EXUPERY

If one is lucky, a solitary fantasy can totally transform one million realities.

Maya Angelou

 Our lives are a reflection of the sensory stimulations around us. We either allow ourselves to be shaped by these stimuli or we shape ourselves through them - transforming external stimuli into a vehicle for our higher growth.

We may at times feel that we are victims of the seemingly uncontrollable circumstances and conditions around us. Yet when we accept that we have control over our own responses to these stimuli, we empower ourselves to initiate action, thereby creating opportunities for influence and opening our flow of positive potential. We take reassurance in knowing that victory often arises from apparent defeat.

There is always an alternative to whatever circumstances we face. Be reminded of your higher self and higher purpose in times of duress and allow them to spot your unique 'window of opportunity'; from there, trust your intuition.

Consider the interconnectedness of all beings and all events. No matter what the circumstances, there is always a 'best move'. After each move, choose a winning move - even if it means losing the game. Your ultimate success lies in your ability to choose your moves wisely rather than accurately. ■

SOWING THE SEEDS OF TRANSFORMING

- Spot opportunities in adversity - make the most of a bad situation.

- Transform your thoughts from uncompassionate and selfish to compassionate and generous.

- Adapt to the situation rather than impose yourself on it.

- Transpose yourself with your adversary - walk in his shoes, empathize with her views.

- Change your mind in a snap! Practice instantaneously releasing anger and attachment.

- Accept defeat and offer victory to those with whom you struggle.

- Replace a bad/negative/angry/selfish thought with a good/positive/kind/generous thought.

- Assist in the transformation of others - make yourself available to be their mirror.

- Learn from your mistakes - ask "What can I learn from this?"

- Exchange roles temporarily with someone else, even if only in your imagination.

Integrity

Live your ethics

truth · consistency · honor

values · apologize · respect

upright · character · honesty · moral

ethical · principled · incorruptible

It's easier to fight for one's principles than to live up to them.
Alfred Adler

The leopard dies but leaves his skin; a man dies but leaves his reputation. *Chinese Proverb*

Don't compromise yourself. You are all you've got.
Janis Joplin

The superior man understands what is right; the inferior understands what will sell.
Confucius

If you think about what you ought to do for other people, your character will take care of itself.
Woodrow Wilson

It's not hard to make decisions when you know what your values are.
Roy Disney

To think is easy. To act is difficult.
To act as one thinks is the most difficult of all.
Johann Wolfgang von Goethe

 Our higher self is inherently authentic and unique, yet most of us succumb to the influences of the conventional beliefs and actions of those around us. Without our own clear grounding, we can become a jumble of the reflected images of others. We must be careful to choose the reflections that complement rather than compete with our authentic self. Complementary choices strengthen our character and the integrity of our authentic self, while competing choices confuse and weaken them.

Being true to your authentic self requires that you live in harmony with your higher self. We sometimes forget who we really are - allowing ourselves to be influenced by how others wish to see us or how our ego wishes us to see ourselves.

We are who we are. It is only our thoughts and actions that lead us astray or lead us towards our goal. The alignment of right action with right thought with higher self produces a truly unstoppable force.

Give yourself the emotional strength to break free from these corrupting influences. Break the urge to seek others' approval, acceptance, and love by reminding yourself of the strength and power of your own self-approval, self-acceptance, and self-love. ■

SOWING THE SEEDS OF INTEGRITY

- Live your values consistently - get to know what you value deeply.

- Commit to honesty - tell the truth (often with extra sensitivity to the feelings of others).

- Maintain a spiritual practice - reflect on that which affirms your deepest values.

- Practice openness in everything - maintain transparency in your motivations.

- Acknowledge your own role in causing pain to others - apologize without reservation.

- Respect life, living things, and their relationships - avoid killing and sexual misconduct.

- Align your actions to be consistent with your ethics - you are your actions.

- Develop your principles and upright character - refrain from immoral and unethical acts.

- Protect and uphold the honor of others - give honor, show honor, attract honor.

- Give your support to people of integrity and leaders of shared values and principles.

Nourishment

Provide for others

reverence for life · healing

sustenance · wholesome · share · flourish

harvest · enrich · hearty · healthy · bounty

nutritious · nutrients · fruits

The true meaning of life is to plant a tree, under whose shade you don't expect to sit. *Nelson Henderson*

Give a man a fish, feed him for a day. Teach him to fish and you feed him for a lifetime.
Native American Saying

Keep your fears to yourself, but share your courage.
Robert Louis Stevenson

THE GREATEST USE OF LIFE IS TO SPEND IT ON SOMETHING THAT WILL OUTLAST IT.
WILLIAM JAMES

Love does not just sit there , like a stone; it has to be made, like bread; remade all the time, made new.
Ursula K. Le Guin

If men believe, as I do, that this present earth is the only heaven, then they will strive all the more to make heaven of it. *Arthur Keith*

Our own health and well being are dependent upon the health and well being of others. We are nourished when we nourish others. This is obvious to most of us, yet we may at times believe that we must hoard for ourselves rather than share with others. We must become convinced that the effects of our actions will outlast even ourselves. We can then reassure ourselves that our higher growth will come from our efforts to grow and to nurture others.

We need not be a parent to love a child nor a farmer to feed the starving. Start by developing your self-concept as a source of nourishment for others. The nourishment we offer others need not be limited to physical and tangible resources, it can take on many forms - knowledge, wisdom, compassion, dedication, love, or care.

Imagine yourself to be a permanent source of nourishment for others, like an oasis in the desert - deep and full of life-giving water - or a shining star that radiates warmth and light in your heart and in your mind. Bring all of the elements together - fire, water, earth, wind and ether - to generate a powerful healing force. Share your healing power with those around you by focusing your nourishing energies on others. ▪

SOWING THE SEEDS OF NOURISHMENT

- Cultivate good seeds in your thoughts and actions - all seeds manifest themselves, good and bad!

- Be a healer - heal the hurt in yourself and others. Share your cures and healing energies with others.

- Share the bounty of your knowledge and other special gifts through teaching.

- Leave only positive impressions behind - leave the world a better place than when you arrived.

- Nurture the causes and conditions that enable yourself and others to blossom.

- Replace unwholesome with wholesome, unhealthy with healthy, and noxious with nutritious.

- Give bountiful and heartfelt appreciation to your parents for giving you life.

- Nourish your relationship with the ones you love - help each other to transform and grow.

- Let your spirit be the sustenance that enriches the spirituality of others.

- Offer nourishment to others - feed the hungry.

Mindfulness

Be aware

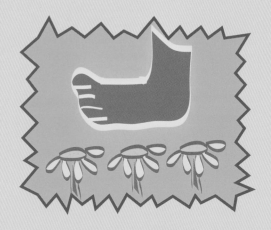

appreciate · conscious · heedful

observing · thoughtful · careful · reflective

remembering · awareness of impact

pure · mindful of all others

Man is a complex being.
He makes deserts bloom and lakes die.
Gil Stern

Whatever is worth doing at all
is worth doing well.
Earl of Chesterfield

**The way to love anything
is to realize that it may be lost.**

G. K. Chesterton

*You will find rest from vanities
if you go about every act in life,
as though it were your last.*
Marcus Aurelius

*There is more to life
than increasing its speed.*

Mahatma Gandhi

Compared to what we ought to be,
we are half awake. *William James*

Look when you look, hear what you hear, taste
what you taste, smell what you smell. *Allan Ginsberg*

 To be fully aware is to be fully alive; to be fully alive is to be fully aware. A life of awareness is rich and robust, replete with majesty and grace. Developing our own awareness directly develops our higher self. Mindfulness is the state of complete awareness of the act or object of attention.

Mindfulness is our lever for self-control. Using it, we can reflect upon and rebuild ourselves to be authentic, consistent, and uncorruptible. Mindfulness need not be developed in a meditation retreat or some distant mountain top. Mindfulness is best practiced through daily living.

Of all actions and habits, developing mindfulness is perhaps the most powerful as a technique for realizing your higher self. Mindfulness practiced together with Attentiveness and Harmony will lead towards the development of all other *Bountiful Behaviors*. These three *Bountiful Behaviors* can become your personal 'triangle of transformation'.

Mindfulness can be developed every minute of every day of your life. Give yourself entirely to what you choose to do; be thoughtful and purposeful in your actions. Be mindful of your interdependence to all things. ■

SOWING THE SEEDS OF MINDFULNESS

- Tune in and stay tuned in - discipline your mind to focus on one thing at a time.

- Come back to the present moment - call yourself back from past reflections and future projections.

- Analyze your feelings; embrace them like a mother holds a baby - study them from this perspective.

- Cultivate a pure and thoughtful mind - meditate daily.

- Reflect on your day and rejoice in the positive changes made - vow to improve even further.

- Consider the necessity of items or actions that may cause harm to others - abstain from those you can.

- Be grateful to those who suffered to provide for your needs - be conscious of your impact.

- Develop mindfulness of others - be thoughtful and purposeful in your actions and their impacts.

- Take time to remember all the living and non-living things that make your life possible.

- Be mindful of your mind - observe the thoughts and feelings that go into and arise from your mind.

Insight

Dissolve wrong perceptions

wisdom · see clearly

deep understanding · *profound*

sagacious · credo · common sense

knowledge · lessons learned

The reasonable man adapts himself to this world; the unreasonable man persists in trying to adapt the world to himself. Therefore, all progress depends on the unreasonable man.

George Bernard Shaw

The secret wants for the insight of eyes unclouded by longing. Those who are bound by desire see only the outward container.

Lau Tzu

An elder in the home is like a treasure.
Chinese Proverb

You are never too old to become younger. *Mae West*

Man's mind once streched by a new idea, never regains its original dimension.

Oliver Wendell Holmes, Jr.

THE LEAST OF THINGS WITH A MEANING IS WORTH MORE IN LIFE THAN THE GREATEST OF THINGS WITHOUT IT.
KARL JUNG

Commonsense is the knack of seeing things as they are, and doing things as they ought to be done. *Calvin E. Stowe*

 Insight strikes us like a bolt of lightning; unmistakable and irrefutable once discovered. Insight puts meaning into our lives; hence by sharing insights, we are helping to put meaning into the lives of others. An insight learned, however, is not easily transferred into a shared insight.

Our basic wiring as human beings seems to require us to experience all insights first-hand. If this is so, each new life must build up its inventory of insights from scratch. If we could rely upon the insights of others, we could perhaps have a greater knowledge base but no greater insights ourselves.

Unfortunately, insights are something that must be experienced individually. Therefore, we need teachers, guides, and facilitators who can master the circumstances in such a way as to allow us to discover our own insights at our own pace.

You can help yourself to increase the quantity and quality of your personal insights by widening your experience of life and by finding and welcoming good teachers. ■

SOWING THE SEEDS OF INSIGHT

- Transcend your pre-existing concepts and dissolve wrong perceptions - take stock of your 'ah-ahs'.

- Accept that you are dying - devote your remaining life, to developing wisdom and compassion.

- Collect your insights and lessons learned - gather up your wisdom as a gift to yourself.

- Interview others for their insights and lessons learned - share your wisdom with each other.

- Protect yourself by protecting others; to protect others you must protect their environment.

- Reflect on the causes of your feelings until you have some insights into what has caused your sufferings.

- Fashion a credo around your special insights to help remember and share them.

- Assume that you may be wrong when in an argument or disagreement - listen attentively.

- Set aside a shelf for books that you find particularly insightful.

- Integrate your personal insights as an illustration - draw it, express it.

Non-Craving

Feel contentment

content · moderation · satisfied

generous · acceptance · abstinence

holdback · self-control · gratified

grateful · happy · fulfilled

Who is content with nothing possesses all things. *Nicolas Bocleau*

A contented mind is a perpetual feast. Chinese Proverb

One can live well even in a palace. *Marcus Aurelius*

I have the greatest of all riches; that of not desiring them. *Eleanora Duse*

Poor is not the person who has too little, but the person who craves more. *Lucius Annaeus Seneca*

PROPERTY GIVEN AWAY IS THE ONLY KIND THAT WILL BE FOREVER YOURS. *MARCUS VALERIUS MARTIALIS*

Most folk are as happy as they make up their minds to be. *Abraham Lincoln*

In this world there are only two tragedies. One is not getting what one wants, and the other is getting it. *Oscar Wilde*

 Intention initiates desire, desire fuels drive, drive engages action. Our desire and drive to realize our higher self is a craving for a spiritual wholeness and as such is inherently good for our health and well being.

The desire and drive to acquire, to consume, and to possess physical or emotional resources lead us towards insecurity and lack of fulfillment. Like drinking salty water, it increases our thirst rather than satisfying it.

Physical sensations are all short-lived. Even if one could string a life-time of pleasing sensations together, each new sensation would have to be greater and more pleasing than the last or a sense of dissatisfaction will arise in spite of the presence of previously pleasant sensations. Pleasantness, like everything else, is relative. We choose its relative center. This means we can define anything as pleasant if we so choose. Therein lies the key to our contentment.

By developing your own contentment without the need to possess the physical and material, you become more satisfied and secure. In turn, this will enable you to feel generous and giving. By refusing to take, you give. By giving, you gain, effortlessly. ■

SOWING THE SEEDS OF NON-CRAVING

- Choose to be content with what you have
  - give thanks for everything.

- Keep your cravings in check by avoiding excesses
  - remember, everything in moderation.

- Shed your addictions; experience abstinence
  for one hour, one day, etc. - kick a bad habit.

- Feel ownership for everything, knowing that
  you ultimately have access to everything you need.

- Cultivate contentment to show your children or
  friends; their fulfillment is a reflection of yours.

- Meditate on wealth, reputation and worldly success;
  see them not as lasting happiness but as impermanent.

- Accept whatever is given to you - do not ask
  "Which will bring me most happiness?"

- Do not haggle - do not ask "What else can I get
  to make me happy?"

- Be generous by giving to others - don't accumulate
  wealth while others starve.

- Restrict the number of choices to be made in a day
  - simplify your life, require less and less each day.

Trustfulness

Keep the faith

faith · trusting · dependable · reliance

consistency · accountable · clear intentions

no doubt · approachable · confident

authentic · trustworthy · mutual

If what you are telling is true, you don't have to choose your words so carefully. *Frank A. Clarke*

The willingness to trust others even when you know you may be taken advantage of is the cornerstone of becoming civilized.

O.A. Battista

No legacy is so rich as honesty.
William Shakespeare

One thousand falsehoods are not as good as one truth. *Chinese Proverb*

It's happier to be sometimes cheated than not to trust. *Samuel Johnson*

I always prefer to believe the best of everybody - it saves so much trouble.
Rudyard Kipling

The man who trusts other men will make fewer mistakes than he who distrusts them will.
Camillo de Cavour

 Our insecurities and fears are deep-rooted in our lack of trust and faith in the world around us. We seek security through faith but may still lack the trust that is necessary for us to be fully open and giving. We can reverse the cycle of insecurity, leading to distrust, leading to fear by being trustful and trustworthy ourselves.

By having faith in ourselves we can extend our faith to others. Modeling the way for our higher selves, each of us can then become a guide; showing others the way forward to their own happiness and well being.

Faith and trust are all that separates happiness from suffering, security from fear, and wisdom from ignorance. Give trust rather than insisting that others earn your trust. Build your faith in the inherent goodness of all beings. As your own faith increases so too does your ability to trust and develop faith in others. ■

SOWING THE SEEDS OF TRUSTFULNESS

- Speak the truth fully and constructively.

- Develop reasons to trust others - start by being trusting of others.

- Hold yourself accountable for your own actions and their consequences.

- Have faith in yourself - show faith in others.

- Overcome self-limiting fears and phobias - radiate confidence by removing your own doubts.

- Be approachable - make it easy for people to want to confide in you.

- Be dependable and reliable - respect others' reliance upon you.

- Act in a manner consistent with your espoused values and advice.

- Protect the confidence that others have entrusted you with.

- Center yourself around the authentic you - let the authentic you shine through.

28 Bountiful Behaviors of
The Gardens of Glorious Living

LEARN – Develop wisdom

Explore your connection	**I**nvestigate Phenomena
Question everything	**Q**uestioning
Open your mind	**U**nderstanding
Reflect and ponder	**E**xamine Deeply
Learn continuously	**N**on-Ignorance
Focus your energy	**C**oncentration
Bow before others	**H**umility

SERVE – Overcome apathy

Share your compassion	**S**ervice
Cherish all equally	**H**armony
Listen with love	**A**ttentiveness
Relieve suffering	**R**elief
Choose to act	**I**ntention
Develop others	**N**urturing
Show goodwill towards all	**G**entleness

ENJOY – Maintain balance

Let go	Detachment
Compose yourself	Inner Stillness
Retain your balance	Middle Way
Live the moment	Present
Cut loose	Laughing Joy
Relax and unwind	Ease
Like yourself	Self-Respect

BESTOW – Offer yourself

Replace harmful with helpful	Transforming
Live your ethics	Integrity
Provide for others	Nourishment
Be aware	Mindfulness
Dissolve wrong perceptions	Insight
Feel contentment	Non-Craving
Keep the faith	Trustful

Seeds of Glorious Living

Words to live by

abstinence	appreciate	cherish
accept	approachable	clear
acceptance	appropriate	clear intent
accomplish	aspire	cognizant
accord	attain	collect
accountable	attempt	comfortable
accrete	attentive	comical
achieve	authentic	commend
acquire	avoid praise	commonsense
act naturally	aware	commute
activate	awareness	compassionate
active	balance	compensate
actualize	begin	complete
adapt	believe	compose
adjust	benevolent	comprehend
admire	benign	conceive
advance	be yourself	confidence
advent	blend	confident
advise	bountiful	confirm
affirm	bow	connect
affirming	bud	conscious
agree	calm	consider
aim	careful	considerate
alert	caring	consistency
alter	catalyst	contemplate
amazing	cause	content
ambition	celebrate	control
amicable	center	convert
amuse	centered-heart	cool
analyze	challenge	cooperate
animate	change	counterweight
apologize	character	courage
apply	check up	course

courteous
credo
cultivate
curious
current
dawn
debate
decisive
dedicate
deep
defer
defuse
deliberate
delicate
delight
dependable
desire
de-stress
develop
devote
diligence
direct
discern
discipline
discover
dispassionate
distinguish
doing
dream
drive
dutiful
educate
effort
elegance
embrace
embrace setbacks
embracing
empathetic
empathize

encourage
endeavor
enduring
energize
energy
engage
enjoy
enlighten
enliven
enrich
equalize
equanimity
escort
ethical
evolve
excite
exercise
exists
expand
experience
experiment
explore
express
fair
faithful
fashion
fathom
feeling
filial
find
first-hand
flourish
focus
forego
foster
fulfilled
funny
further
gather

generate
generous
give
gladness
glean
glide
graceful
grateful
gratified
gratitude
growing
guiding
happiness
happy
harvest
healing
healthy
hearty
heedful
helpful
helping
here and now
hold back
honesty
honor
hope
humble
humorous
illuminating
impartial
impel
impress
improvise
in the moment
inception
incorruptible
inform
initiate
inquire

inquisitive
insightful
inspect
inspire
intelligent
intent
interdependence
intermediate
investigate
kind
knowing
knowledgeable
laugh
lead
learn continuously
let go
like yourself
listening
live
look critically
look deeply
look into
loose
love all
magical
marvel
meaningful
meet other's needs
mend
mentor
merriment
metamorphosis
mild
mindful
miraculous
modeling
moderate
moderation
modest

modify
moral
motion
motivate
muse
mutual
neutral
no boasting
no doubt
no extremes
no worries
non-agitated
non-grasping
non-judgemental
notice
nourish
now
nutrient
nutritious
observant
observing
offer
open-minded
origin
originate
overture
passage
patience
pause
peaceful
pensive
perceptive
perseverence
persistent
pilot
pity
placid
play
polite

ponder
positive potential
praise
preface
present
principled
produce
profound
progress
prostrate
protect
prove for yourself
purify
purpose
put to use
question
questioning
reach for the stars
ready
realize
reap
reawake
receptive
recharge
reclaim
recognize
reconcile
reflect
reflective
reform
refresh
regard
regenerate
rehearse
reinvigorate
rejoice
rejuvenate
relax
release

reliance
relieve
relinquish
relish
remembering
remove obstacles
reopen
replace
replenish
resolute
respect
rest
restore
revel
reverence for life
revive
revolutionize
ridiculous
right tension
rouse
route
sagacious
satisfied
search
see clearly
seek wisdom
self-accepting
self-control
self-esteem
sensational
sense
sensitive
serene
set one's sight on
share
sharing
shepherd
show
simple

simplicity
smile
soft touch
solitude
source
spark
spiritual
spontaneous
spur
start
steer
step back
steward
still
stir
subordinate self
substantiate
support
sustain
sustenance
sympathize
synthesize
tame
target
temper
tender-hearted
tender
test
thankful
thanks
think
thoughtful
tolerance
trail
train
tranquil
transcend
transition
transmute

treasure
trust
trusting
trustworthy
truth
try
unassuming
unfold
unlock
unprejudiced
unpretentious
unruffled
unwind
upright
use
usher
validate
value
vary
view
vigilant
vitalize
volunteer
want
wholesome
will
willful
wise
wish
wonder
yearn
yield
zen
zestful

About the Author

Know the source

Steve Morris was born and raised in Virginia, USA. The son of a would-be Catholic priest and his Irish Catholic bride, he was reared in a traditional Catholic fashion - baptism, confession, confirmation - even serving as an altar boy at daily mass.

As a rebellious teenager, Steve broke away from his Roman Catholic roots and began a twenty-five year search for a spiritual reconnection. Attracted by the strong humanist values of Christianity but repelled by the dogma of divine determinism, Steve went from Christian faith to faith until he was left with almost no faith at all!

After relocating to Asia in 1989, he was exposed to the multitude and diversity of religious and spiritual beliefs of the Eastern world. Here, he would eventually come to experience the teachings of Buddhism and of Tibetan Buddhism in particular through contacts with some of its great spiritual teachers, including His Holiness the Dalai Lama.

Steve noticed what many other students of comparative religious philosophy have, that there are many common values held by most religions. *Glorious Living!* is an effort to put forth a model set of behaviors that will benefit anyone, regardless of their faith. Additional thoughts and experiences are shared at www.gloriousliving.org

In 1998 he founded Steve Morris Associates to coach organizational leaders to improve the quality of worklife for themselves, their teams, and their communities. In this capacity he draws on his more than twenty years of experience working with hundreds of organizations and leaders throughout the world. To find out more about his work in this regard, visit www. stevemorrisassociates.com

While *Glorious Living!* is Steve's first published book, he has been a prolific writer of news and magazine articles and is a frequent television, radio and conference speaker on topics of leadership, teamwork, self-development and quality of worklife. Contact *www.aspire.com.sg* for more information on engaging Steve as a conference speaker or to check on upcoming events and publications. ■

May any small merit

arising from

the Sowing of these

Seeds of Glorious Living

be dedicated to

the attainment

of happiness

and well being of all beings.